Superhuman Revolution

A Guide to Thriving in the Age of Advanced Intelligence

DR. Selva Sugunendran

CEng, MIEE, MCMI, CHt, MIMDHA, MBBNLP, MGO¬NLP, DBS

AI Robotics Strategist & Visionary Author, #1 Best Selling Author, Speaker & Coach

Website: Https://AIRoboticsForGood.com

Email: Selva@AIRoboticsForGood.com

Hello & Welcome!

If you have been looking at the title of the book, let me say, any of the following titles would apply to the contents of this book:

BOOK TITLES:

1. "Superhuman Era: Preparing for the Future of Human Evolution"

2. "Beyond Humanity: Navigating the Rise of Superhumans"

3. "Superhumans vs. Humans: Embracing the Next Frontier"

4. "The Superhuman Frontier: Opportunities and Dangers Ahead"

5. "Superhuman Revolution: A Guide to Thriving in the Age of Advanced Intelligence"

All these titles emphasise the radical newness of the technologies associated with AI.

It is a comprehensive study of the issues – and, more importantly, of the opportunities – presented by superhuman technologies and how we, as humans, can navigate them. The complexity of the issues, technological and humanistic, has eluded scholars in a multitude of disciplines and this book makes your path easier to navigate.

Contents

About The Author

DR. Selva is an AI Robotics Strategist & visionary Author. He is also a #1 Best Selling Author, Speaker and Coach.

DR SELVA SUGUNENDRAN has performed many lofty positions in life, The most uplifting to him is the one he chose, which was to serve mankind by showing them the way to health, wealth, and success.

Upon selling his UK based Integrated High Security IT company which he ran for 25 years as the company owner, he took the "jump" out of the corporate world into his passion for helping people to be more, do more and get more out of their life than they ever thought possible! Young or old, he helped them create a new blueprint for life that literally changed their world and continues to do so.

As a result of that work, he was attracted to study, research, write and publish 50+ books of which 6 books were #1 Best Sellers in genres Health & Wellness, Alzheimer's / Dementia, Success in Business &Life, and Christianity & more recently on AI & Robotics

He has developed a special Ai- Robotic Machine (which is currently in a prototype stage) which can be used as a "Virtual Carer" for Dementia patients who live alone and cannot afford 24-hour care.

He has published several books on AI Robotics. These include the following: ***"AI For Beginners", "Rogue AI-The Oppenheimer Effect", "Mastering the minds of machines", "AI Trilogy, AI Game Changers", "AI and its Trajectory"*** and ***"Superhuman Revolution-A Guide to Thriving in the age of Advanced Intelligence."***

Foreword

It is a great privilege to bring to you a book on this most crucial and most important of questions: what will it mean to be human in the coming age of the superhuman? It is also a duty.

This book, Superhumans vs Humans: Embracing the Next Frontier by DR. Selva who is an AI Robotics Strategist and Visionary author, is a comprehensive study of the issues – and, more importantly, of the opportunities – presented by superhuman technologies and how we, as humans, can navigate them. The complexity of the issues, technological and humanistic, has eluded scholars in a multitude of disciplines. The author has combined insights from no fewer than six such disciplines to provide in this book a roadmap on how best to grasp them.

As a practitioner of an emerging field – 'AI ethics and human enhancement' – the rate of change is impressive. What was once the premise of a Philip K Dick novel now heralding a rapidly approaching, technologically enhanced future of brain-computer interfaces, genetic modification and artificial intelligence environments. Curing disease, extending the human lifespan and enhancing minds beyond our natural human abilities now seem like tangible possibilities instead of mysterious, far-off dreams. Yet with this rapid change comes great danger. We cannot continue to plough ahead at this rate unless we take the time to think through the huge ethical, social and philosophical questions that will need to be addressed if, when and how these solutions are implemented.

He approaches these issues with a seriousness and a sympathy that make the book a convincing and moving read. His history of AI over the decades, from its inceptive years to today's hot-off-the-press technologies, offers practical benchmarks for how we got where we are today, while painstaking details about each of the three key technologies — neural interfaces, biotechnology, and robotics — that could give rise to superhumans, show both their promise and their difficulties.

One of the great successes of this book is its even-handed discussion of the ethical and moral questions raised by human enhancement. Bostrom does not dodge the big questions about the nature of selfhood, equity and what makes us human, but tackles them systematically, while also giving a clear-eyed view of the potential benefits, as well as the dangers. The chapters on regulatory frameworks and the need for robust forms of governance are particularly welcome, with suggestions for how the governance of superhuman tech could be used to promote positive ends.

The chapters on the social and political consequences of superhumans are thought-provoking too. He points out the potential for lucrative new forms of inequality and stratification and offers some sensible policy recommendations for boosting inclusive growth. He emphasises the need to get many more people and workplaces ready for the future by supporting lifelong learning and skills. If this happens, he suggests, people committing suicide for not having a job in a superhuman world could be a very distant memory indeed.

Similarly, the book delves into how enhanced humanity could govern. For instance, superhuman leaders with bio or cyber augmentations could make better decisions and efficiently tackle complex social problems, but this will require new models of governance, enabled by algorithmic transparency and openness to share responsibilities in the decision-making process. Will Wood's vision for how we can learn to better engage with each other and foster a collective approach to governance is an interesting blueprint for how augmentation could be applied in a way that benefits everyone.

Moving forward, it is crucial that we continue to strive for the creation of resilient societies. Not least, this would help reduce pressures and the market for drugs that, in turn, could provide a robust moral foundation for the initiatives we are beginning to develop. It is an urgent matter that should inspire global collaborations of the kind that Bostrom and Ord call for: 'We need international standards for the regulation of human enhancement technologies. This is a global challenge best met through worldwide co-operation.' But it is nothing less than a global challenge, a matter for all of humanity, and not one that we can hope to meet unless we start

Overall, "**Superhuman Revolution-A Guide to Thriving in the age of Advanced Intelligence**" is required reading for all interested in preparing for the near human future. It should be compulsory reading in a wide range of courses for policymakers, technologists, educators and, indeed, all who are concerned citizens. As Curze notes in his concluding chapter, Daland and Galli: 'get right down to the most practical of recommendations … and offer proposals for distributing the emergent opportunities and responsibilities.' Thanks to Curze's insightful engagement of these authors, we are more capable of mastering the unfolding realities of human enhancement. Hopefully, we bequeath to our descendants a future of wiser, more wholesome enhancement.

I am certain this book will be widely used to comprehend the unprecedented transitions ahead and to help navigate building a future in which superhuman technologies expand our collective humanity. We must co-create and inhabit that future together, guided by the same ethical imperatives and the same goals of the common good. As a species, let us create our next horizon with open minds and open hearts and reap the benefits for all.

By DR. Janet Thompson

Introduction:
The Dawn of Superhumans

Standing as we do on the verge of the most profound period of change since the advent of agriculture some 10,000 years ago (or of the internet, which spawned a tsunami of other change after its emergence in the mid-1990s), it's easy to vacillate between the optimism that animated McLuhan and his successors, and a sense of anxiety and pessimism – of deep trepidation – for what the future holds.

The Ontario writer and journalist Douglas Coupland was both prescient and farsighted when he boasted that he could 'predict your new eyes' in a series of articles he authored for Newsweek magazine and subsequently assembled into the book Kittens, God and Why You Don't Have a Clue (2006). Coupland was writing as a member of Generation X, caught between the baby boomers and his children's cohort, Generation Y. At the time, his concerns were minimal. He opined that: 'True, computers and the internet might steal an average of five hours per day from everyone, but in that new free time people seem happier, more adept in relationships, and more given to gracious volunteer work.' And typically for someone in tune with the zeitgeist, Coupland was correct. In the 90s, he took Internet Tickertape, a play, and transformed it into Micro serfs (1995), a witty novel about twentysomethings working for Microsoft on an impulse project – no one can remember its exact nature.

Once the domain of sci-fi monsters and spandex-clad superheroes, superhumans are finally emerging from the pages of comic books and movie screens. A convergence of AI, biotechnology, neural augmentation and robotics is now coming to fruition in man-machine hybrids that transcend the limits of normal humans. Superhumans with enhanced physical, cognitive and sensory capabilities are poised to reshape our world according to rules that we are only beginning to grasp. We need to prepare for what lies ahead – both the rewards and the risks.

Machines vs. Humans:
A Shifting Paradigm

In popular discussion of AI and robotics for decades, there has been a clear antagonism dangled between man and machine. While this kind of binary approach to the subject is still useful, raising important ethical and pragmatic issues, it's discourse that's increasingly unfit to describe the latest shift in our interconnected relationship with technology. A growing fuzziness dividing human and machine is blurring the boundaries between us and our tools, in favour of a hybridity in which our biology and our technology are one.

And now we see the development of AI systems that can outperform humans at playing chess and other games, as well as diagnosing diseases and finding new knowledge. However, these systems for now are constrained by the directions they are programmed with, and by their inability to think outside the box. What is the next step? It is to integrate AI systems into the human body and mind, to modify humans to become both superhumans who can utilise the precision and speed of AI as well as their own abilities to think creatively and to combine verbal and other abilities in harnessing their emotions.

Purpose of the Book:
Guiding Humanity through the Transformation

Superhumans vs. Humans: Preparing for the Era of Superman Technology provides a detailed roadmap for responding to the radical change that superhuman technology will bring to us all. The book isn't speculative history or science fiction: it is designed to be a practical handbook for individuals, communities and policymakers to survive and even thrive in a superhuman world.

The chapters that follow will examine different aspects of this transition and offer both insights and techniques on how to make the most of the opportunities and minimise harm. We will examine the technologies at the forefront of the shift to superhumanity, from neural interfaces that augment cognition to genetic technologies that prolong human lifespan and consider what they must teach us about human identity and morality. We will grapple with deep queries, including: what is it to be human? Is human life fair? What is to be done?

One of the core conclusions of this book is that superhuman technologies are double-edged: used right, they will cut through most current challenges of healthcare, education and defence, leading to radical improvements in quality of life and societal resilience. Taken as a whole, these advancements may have a profoundly transformative effect on what it means to be human. However, if superhuman technologies are deployed inappropriately or inequitably, they will cut into the social fabric, further entrenching social inequalities and leading to new forms of warfare.

Embracing Opportunities, Mitigating Risks

We need to help others translate the above scenarios into a world that is understandable, vibrant and empowering so that we can make collectively wise, robust and adoptive decisions. We must make sure that technological innovation is not dictated by elites or necessarily leading to a world where many are left out. Instead, by having informed and involved debate now, we will be able to select the best possible path to superhumanity – one in which it benefits all of us.

There will be dramatic changes in everything from education systems (if future generations learn how to learn with brain-boosting smart drugs or with 'augmented tutors'), to workplaces (what will it mean to be a superhuman in a factory?) and social institutions (what kinds of norms will people live by, in a culture shaped by converging and increasingly superhuman lives?).

A Call to Action

This book is an invitation to anyone who would like to participate in shaping that future together – technologist and teacher, policymaker and voter alike. I hope it will provide you with ideas of what's possible, and with tools to design your own future and make it happen.

In setting out this way, let's recall that the future does not exist as a destination (and the way we imagine it does not do us many favours). Instead, what we move into is created by our choices and how we act. We should try to do that next frontier with foresight, intelligence and compassion – so that when superhumans come, they bring a new wave of human excellence and human progress.

The chapters that follow dive deeper into this transformation, providing a map for the journey ahead: a path toward a tomorrow of coexistence, cooperation and co-flourishing between superhumans and humans alike.

1

The Rise Of Super Humans

Evolution of AI:
From Machines to Superhumans

The story of how we got from simple machines to AI and deep neural networks is one of the most intriguing sagas in the history of technology. Some of the earliest machines with any hint of the intelligence possessed by modern systems were the ancient abacus, and simple automata such as the Antikythera mechanism from around 150 BCE. The rise of digital computers in the middle of the 20th century and their ultimate evolution to AI came on the heels of several decades of vital and often overlooked advances in mathematics and computer science. Initially, these systems could do only very specific tasks that had been programmed in advance. However, in just a matter of decades, Moore's law has simultaneously provided massive increases in computing power and data, and rapid advances in algorithmic sophistication have allowed AI to enter new domains previously seen as exclusive to humans.

Over the past couple of decades, we have seen AI systems that can process huge quantities of information, learn from experience and, most significantly, develop emergent capabilities such as pattern recognition, decision-making, and even creativity. This has let us start on the long journey towards the development of superhumans – machines that merge the calculation and raw processing power of AI with the flexibility and empathy of humans.

Key Technologies Driving the Change

This allows us to identify the main drivers of the rise of the superhuman. The three key technologies that are converging to enhance the human are neural interfaces, biotechnology, and robotics.

Neural interfaces, such as brain-computer interfaces (BCIs), represent a new frontier in human augmentation because they provide a more direct conduit between the brain and its surroundings by transmitting information via permanent implanted electrodes or light-activated sensors called optogenetic switches. That means that, rather than interacting with the material world through sensory perception and motor behaviour, it will be possible to control machines simply by thinking about them and having sensory impressions fed from those machines back into your brain. BCIs promise to restore the ability to walk for the paralysed, boost memory and cognition, and even facilitate telepathic communication – something that Neuralink and other companies are currently trying to achieve by fusing AI directly with the brain.

Biotechnology is yet another vital pillar of the superhuman evolutionary pavement. Recent advances in genetic engineering such as CRISPR-Cas9 could allow us to edit the human genome at the base-pair level to remove almost all genetic diseases, enhance physical and mental traits, and extend lifespans. In short, there is now a powerful plausibility to the claim that in the not-too-distant future we might all generate superhuman offspring.

Robotics, combined with developments in AI, is making our musculoskeletal system, our huge interface to the physical world, more capable. Exoskeletons and prosthetics, with AI-enacted myoelectric control, are amplifying human power and finesse. They allow humans – including some disabled and   including increasingly capable non-disabled individuals – to do things a human alone can't. It's not far from there to producing superhumans: humans amplified and extended by AI-enacted improvements to their innate capabilities.

Defining Superhumans: Capabilities and Potential

Superhumans of this sort are natural humans who have significantly empowered their physical, cognitive and sensory capabilities via technology-based enhancements.

Physical: Superhuman strength, speed and stamina are just a matter of hormone infusions and organ reconstruction based on compatible genetic traits that we already know about but can't access because our genome is locked by our parents' DNA. Hybrid traits – part human and part machine, part organic and part inorganic – may then become the accepted reality. Muscle and bone extensions are one possibility, though enhancements that transcend contemporary medical possibilities would likely involve exoskeleton walkers and AI-controlled low-level prosthetics. Ultimately, the organisms involved could look and function in ways that are difficult to discern from either exclusively organic or purely inorganic creations.

Cognitive enhancements: Integration of AI with the human brain via neural interfaces could enhance memory, speed up learning processes, and make us better at solving problems. People could access an endless amount of information instantly, communicate in different languages, or perform mathematical tasks that would now be a tall order for sophisticated calculators or computers. Such cognitive superhumans could excel in any area of intellectual engagement, from scientific research to military and political strategies.

Sensory augmentation: Sensory enhancements might grant superhumans perceptual capacities outside natural human ranges. Enhanced eyesight might permit vision via infrared or ultraviolet light or into very low (or very high) light levels. Enhanced hearing might permit sounds of ultrasonic and infrasonic frequencies.

Such sensory augmentation would enhance everyone's sensitivities beyond measures of 'normal human functioning' and would permit novel modes of interaction with the natural environment.

Possibilities and Potential Implications: There are vast possibilities and implications of superhuman capabilities. We can imagine superhumans speeding the diagnosis and treatment of disease, enabling us to move toward personalised medicine, where we tailor treatment to each patient's unique biochemical makeup. We can envision superhuman learning creating a generation of students capable of absorbing and using knowledge at exponentially growing rates. We can think of superhumans turbo-charging innovation, productivity and efficiency, providing fruitful returns to economic growth and societal enrichment in the workforce.

But along with the promise of superhumans come a slew of ethical, social, political and philosophical challenges. If we can eradicate traits such as disease, greed or fear, what does it mean to be a human being – and what kinds of questions and capabilities will such enhancements bring to light? If superhuman progress is unevenly distributed across social and geographic borders, what does this mean for the young and fragile political project of globalisation? How do we avoid superhumans becoming super elites to the detriment of their fellow 'ordinary' citizens? What safeguards are needed to avoid technology becoming a tool of oppression and, alternatively, what limits should scientific research have in its search to develop new technologies? And what happens to our autonomy, privacy and sense of self with the usage of these new technologies?

But as we look upon this emerging frontier, it is vital that we can foresee and take responsibility when facing these challenges. The capability of integrating AI and human augmentation, offers not only boundless opportunities but also ramifications beyond the scope of one individual with capabilities enhanced by technologies.

The questions that need to be answered with greater certainty are the ethical questions, the social questions, and the practical questions about how to enable superhumans to generate a positive future for themselves, and for all humans. We will address these questions in our remaining chapters. If we understand the causal structure that precipitates the superhuman era, and we anticipate many of the consequences of being superhumans, then the outcome should be a more level playing field for all humans. It is to our advantage to embrace the only unstoppable, inevitable future that we can see.

2

The Benefits of Superhuman Integration

Enhanced Human Abilities:
Physical and Cognitive Augmentations

But over the next century, as mankind finally sets out to become less than human, and more truly than human, the prospect of connecting advanced technologies to the human body and brain could be unprecedentedly liberating. Even in this early phase, the most obvious manifestation of the superhuman is likely to be a significant augmentation to physical, mental and cognitive capabilities. But this kind of enhancement could radically reshape human experience in countless arenas – from health and vitality to general productivity to human achievement itself.

Physical Augmentations: The combination of robotics and biotechnology will dramatically enhance human physical abilities. For example, exoskeletons can provide users with superhuman strength and stamina, allowing them to perform tasks that require massive physical labour with ease. These suits are already used in different industrial workplaces to help workers lift heavy objects without a strain, thereby increasing efficiency and safety.

And not only can new prosthetic devices restore lost human functions, but they can also improve on them. The latest prosthetic limbs with AI-driven neural interfaces can move in a very similar way to human ones. Moreover, users of advanced prosthetic limbs can often exercise greater control over their movements and achieve greater precision than with their biological appendage. This control is becoming more and more like a natural extension of the user's nervous system.

In addition to prosthetic enhancements and exoskeletons which aim to augment human physical functions mechanically, genetic engineering might one day empower us to achieve our physical goals at a biological level. Using new precise genetic-editing tools such as CRISPR-Cas9, at least some of our genetic disorders might one day be removed, and traits including muscle mass, endurance and even resistance to diseases could all be amplified. The outcome might be a new 'athletic' type of human, whose physical capabilities would make them vastly more efficient. Sport, health and the everyday world may take on a very different aspect.

Cognitive Enhancements: In the cognitive domain, AI and neural interfaces are likely to interact initially in reciprocal ways that could bring about profound changes in how humans' function. Brain-computer interfaces (BCIs) are systems that enable a brain to connect and communicate directly with an external device. They would allow for seamless communication between a machine and a brain through a direct interface, enabling someone using a brain-computer interface (and maybe soon, standard computerised education) to retrieve and process information at record speeds, providing unprecedented cognitive enhancements and learning capabilities.

The most tantalising application of the BCIs could be in the realm of education – if they augment cognitive functions, they could help students diverge, enriching the learning experience. Imagine pupils who can instantly access databases of information, conduct complex counts and calculations, and communicate in any language at a moment's notice. These are not just opportunities for individual learning, but for the global innovation and creativity of mass dissemination.

In the workplace in particular, cognitive enhancements would enhance productivity gains among professionals. Researchers, engineers and finance professionals would all benefit from improved memory, analysis and decision-making skills. Progress would be accelerated, and new horizons opened, as a result.

Superhumans in Healthcare: Revolutionizing Medicine

The convergence of superhuman technologies with healthcare can bring about a profound change in the field, creating better outcomes for patients, more personalised and effective treatments, and a more efficient healthcare system. Better treatments and diagnostics will come from superhuman abilities.

- **Advanced Diagnostics:** AI diagnostic tools are already being designed to 'read X-rays better than any human clinician', and more generally surpass human doctors by compiling masses of data and identifying aberrations from patterns others miss. AI-driven platforms to detect disease – in some cases, such as cancers, potentially at an earlier stage than current human diagnosis – already exist. Consider, further, that, integrated with a BCIs, such tools could work in real time to track health and gather diagnostics leading to individuals self-managing their own health earlier and better.

- **Personalised medicine:** Due to the availability of genetic engineering and AI-based analysis, gene modifications can correct for hereditary illnesses, and detailed analysis of patients' genetics and health can track a patient's condition over time and suggest personalised treatment plans based on an individual's situation. Such treatments can be targeted to their genetic and health conditions, leading to effective treatments with fewer negative side effects. This approach also eliminates much trial and error that vectors in conventional medicine commonly incorporate to find a workable treatment.

- **Super Therapies:** Innovative therapies are the third potential class of accelerated change, ones that have hitherto been impossible, or thought to be impossible. For example, with superhuman technologies, it is possible to develop treatments for previously incurable neurological conditions, with neural interfaces being developed to stimulate specific brain regions to restore lost functions that are responsible for them, such as for Parkinson's disease, epilepsy and spinal cord injury. In the future, it may be possible to develop neural implants that restore lost cognitive abilities in people who have neurodegenerative disease.

Economic Impact:
New Industries and Opportunities

Superhumans will also spark whole new industries and economic opportunities, stimulating growth and innovation across the economy. As superhuman technologies gradually seep into the economy, they will foster demand for new products, services and expertise that would create jobs while spawning new sectors of business.

- **Technology creation and manufacturing:** The technologies that are available for making people superhuman – neural interfaces, prosthetics, genetic engineering tools – must be designed and built. People specialising in technology creation and manufacturing (researchers, engineers and technicians) would need to focus on this domain, delivering the next wave of innovation and economic growth. Further, the production of these technologies would drive an increase in demand for materials, components and manufacturing equipment, creating another economic stimulus.

- **Healthcare and biotechnology:** Continuing the point above, this area will expand dramatically as superhuman technologies are more and more incorporated into medical practice. Especially, new kind of healers will be also needed to serve patients with skill sets trained in used of advanced diagnostic tools, individualised drugs, and new modalities of therapeutic interventions. In addition, biotech enterprises will spearhead the creation and commercialisation of genetic engineering and 'next generation' augmentation, therefore creating jobs and economic value.

- **Education and Training:** A proliferation of cognitive enhancements will create a demand for educational programmes for teaching people how to gain advantage from these transformative technologies. In turn, these breakthroughs will transform classrooms, changing the way people learn. As people need to continuously update their skill sets, in addition to the current importance of lifelong learning, demand for education and training services will expand. Demand for teachers, trainers and administrators will increase.

Conclusion:
A New Frontier of Human Potential

Superhuman technologies would enable people to run faster and strengthen their muscles far beyond current limits. It might enable us to send people into space without spacesuits. It will enable us to fix genetic problems like blindness and deafness, micro size our cameras and read books anywhere. We should use the benefits that superhuman technologies will provide us.

However, it is vital that we carefully consider the ethical, social and practical implications of superhuman abilities. From increasing equality now to enabling empowerment of people with more disabilities in the future, the capability impacts will be significant.

If superhumans are the future, then new collaborations and professions will arise. But the innovation of new technologies should be accompanied by the innovation of new opportunities to access and use those technologies, in healthy and moral ways. The good news is this exciting new frontier for human potential is only just beginning.

3

Ethical and Moral Considerations

The Ethics of Augmentation:
Where to Draw the Line

For better or worse, the future will belong to superhumans. Much will depend on the answers we give to a series of related, complex ethical questions. But the most pressing, and important, ethical question concerns the extent and style of human enhancement. Many people accept that humans should use biotechnologies such as prosthetics and neural interfaces to enhance the quality of life and health of people with disabilities, such as those living with MS or paralysis – or even those who are simply missing a digit or two.

The most controversial application of the technology might be to effectively 'transcend' human nature entirely by using genetic modifications to enhance physical and cognitive capacities beyond the natural human range. Curing all cases of hereditary disease is, generally, welcomed. Enhancing intelligence, muscular strength or aesthetic features creates a clear downside because it could well segregate society into enhanced 'Normals Plus' and less enhanced 'Naturals' who are riven with resentment. Enhanced people might have an efficient and decisive advantage over Naturals – cementing existing social divisions and transforming them into a stratified society of upgraded overlords.

Moral Implications:
What It Means to Be Human

Superhumans bring to the forefront certain questions that have always existed but that will become more pressing and more transformative in our lives. We are forced to rethink what it means to be human. Traditional ideas about humans, like intelligence, emotional richness, bipedalism, two eyes, two hands, and so on, will no longer be what they are now. By augmenting ourselves, we will become something different. And the question is: what kind of moral difference does it make?

For example, if cognitive enhancements enable people to perceive things at much greater speed, or to process information and solve problems in leaps and bounds compared with others, they might alter how we see notions of merit or achievement: perhaps enhanced people end up being regarded not as 'just' human, but as somehow distinct from, and possibly superior to, un-augmented humans; we might have to rethink our notion of equality and fairness. This muddying of our sense of identity is another potential consequence. Not to render help, but to enhance When a human becomes an enhanced version of themselves, how will we feel about those who have not adopted the enhancements? Will they feel lesser or deficient in some way?

And there's a consent issue, too, since superhuman abilities could be inherited by descendants who didn't consent to such changes. Future generations might have scant choice about being born with genetic additions that they didn't consent to – and legitimate worries about rights to originality or sovereignty over one's biological inheritance.

Regulatory Frameworks: Establishing Boundaries

Figuring out how to cope with these ethical difficulties will require strong regulatory frameworks that spell out what new enhancement technologies may and may not do. Such frameworks need to be created before or as the technologies become available. It is important that they make the application of these technologies follow social and ethical norms, rather than breaking down societal structures. They should bolster the inclusiveness of society by ensuring that new technologies are not the exclusive preserve of a genetically or technology-enhanced elite.

However, it is done, regulations must also ensure effective protection against misuse, inefficiency and harm. This will be especially true when it comes to oversight of neural interface and other augmentation trials, informed consent and long-term study of enhanced individuals to assess for side-effects and unexpected consequences.

Establishing these frameworks will require international cooperation, because technological progress is increasingly global – an enhancement developed in one part of the world can begin to spread through the global technological hivemind almost instantly. That means that a coordinated global effort will be necessary to ensure that ethical standards are not relaxed in a mad dash to the bottom, where countries compete to see who can provide the most permissive settings for enhancement technologies.

4

The Role of Superhumans in Defence

Superhuman Soldiers:
Enhancing Military Capabilities

Military forces are at the vanguard of technological trends, and superhuman technology is no different. Giving soldiers superhuman powers would transform the nature of combat, conferring powerful strategic advantages. Metahuman soldiers might become more powerful, faster or more resistant than the soldiers they will face.

Exoskeletons allowing soldiers to carry greater burdens or move faster or survive harsher climates are one thing, but neural interfaces that enhance their situational awareness and decision-making capabilities – by letting them read, process and respond to hastened streams of battlefield information – would likely be even more impactful. New aspects of physical and cognitive enhancement might radically alter the paradigms of armed conflict.

Ethical Warfare: Dilemmas of Enhanced Soldiers

The prospective benefits of super-men are obvious but, as soldiers, their use would also raise profound questions of ethics. In the quest for military superiority, gruff and gritty soldiers could become dehumanised warriors, puppets of enhanced physical and psychological power commanded by zealous forces. The grey zone of man/machine continues – as do our dilemmas of fighting ethically.

Developing superhuman soldiers might also cause an arms race, where nations compete with one another to produce ever more superhuman enhancements, increasing the probability of conflict and greater global instability. Most importantly, how would we treat enduring superhuman soldiers after their active service? World governments would need to ensure that such soldiers are reintegrated back into society and that they receive adequate support and treatment for any physical and psychological conditions that may have arisen from the enhancements.

Safeguards Against Rogue Superhumans

A constant worry about super soldiers is that they will go rogue: the traits that make them valuable fighting machines are also dangerous traits if they find their way into the wrong hands or do things against their programming.

Countering this risk will require rigorous layers of control and safeguards – such as stringent vetting and training protocols, rigorous monitoring of augmentees, and robust deactivation and containment protocols if violence ensues. International law and cooperation will be key to avoiding 'super-soldier' misuse and to ensuring that augmentation serves the common good.

Building some of these in safeguards will require developing completely secure remote control and monitoring capability for superhuman soldiers – not to mention fail-safe options so that enhancements can be turned off if necessary. In turn, creating a culture of ethical responsibility in the military may have to involve incentivising everybody to use superhuman soldiers in ways that accord with humanitarian principles and international law.

5

Social Impact and Inequality

Addressing the Digital Divide: Ensuring Equal Access

In the wrong hands, the application of superhuman technologies might exacerbate existing social inequalities. Here the divide between those who have access to modern forms of information and communication technology, and those who do not, might find its counterpart in the human-augmentation domain. From the outset, we should strive to make enhancements available to all, regardless of socioeconomic status, to prevent the emergence of a new elite class of superhumans.

What's needed is policies and programmes to enhance access to enhancement technologies. Governments should subsidise certain essential enhancements, as is done with drug insurance for low-income Canadians, and provide public funding for research and development. Education and awareness programmes can help fill the gap too and help ensure marginalised groups aren't left behind in the next technological revolution.

Superhumans and Social Stratification: Bridging the Gap

But the rise of superhumans might also bring new forms of social stratification, in which enhanced individuals experience significant advantages over others who find themselves on the other side of a technological divide – such as better access to employment, education or healthcare.

Existing to fill this gap is the promotion of values such as inclusive policies that give the same human rights and opportunities to people with and without enhancement, to protect the rights of those 'naturals', as well as anti-discrimination laws, particularly those outlawing employment discrimination, and respect for diversity.

Moreover, encouraging plurality of approaches in the development and use of superhuman technologies could reduce or prevent potentially detrimental social divides. If more people are engaged in the creation and deployment of such technologies, the designs are more apt to consider how the technologies can benefit a wide variety of communities, and to provide safeguards that many people would require. Such an approach to the emergence of superhuman technologies could lead to greater inclusivity and parity, so that the benefits of these technologies reach as many people as possible, not just a select few.

Policy Recommendations for Inclusive Growth

It will be up to policymakers to promote superhuman growth that entails inclusive growth, through regulatory regimes that maximise equitable access, preserve individual rights and encourage innovation.

Key policy recommendations include:

- **Subsidising Enhancement Technologies:** Supporting subsidies or public funding schemes for making key enhancement technologies affordable and widely available.

- **Anti-Discrimination Laws:** Passing and enforcing laws that protect persons against discrimination based on EE status.

- **Education and Training Funding** for education and training programmes that get workers ready for a world with lots of new technology.

- **Public Awareness Campaigns:** This involves collective efforts to promote awareness on benefits and harms/risks of superhuman technologies, to enable people to make knowledge-based and wise decisions.

- **International Cooperation:** Encouraging international collaboration to develop international standards and ethical codes for enhancement technology development and use.

What is more, governments and private companies can co-develop programmes that promote inclusivity in shaping the future of far-reaching, superhuman technologies. For instance, public-private partnerships can be set up to fund innovation and development, and community engagement programmes can be designed to give the concerns and perspectives of marginalised groups the weight they deserve.

6

Education and Workforce Transformation

Redefining Education:
Preparing for a Superhuman Future

We will not prepare our students to enter a world of superhumans if we continue to train them through systems that value rote memorisation and high-stakes testing.

We will also need to educate students differently – so that we are not just churning out regurgitators. Students will have to be taught the fundamental and necessary skills of critical thinking, creativity and the ability to cope with change – skills that will be required in an AI and post-human future in which we use more technologies like AI tutors, augmented reality and so on to create more immersive and personalised learning practices.

Furthermore, educational structures must encourage widening the scope of lifelong learning so that individuals can readily upgrade their skillsets and retrain as the pace of technological progress escalates. This will entail educational structures that are flexible and accessible through extended and more flexible engagement with undergraduate and graduate courses, online learning and micro-credentialing as well as vocational and skills education programmes. This will promote a culture of lifelong learning so that people are primed to capitalise on the far-reaching challenges and opportunities of the superhuman age.

Workforce Evolution: New Skills and Jobs

The impact of superhuman technologies on the workforce will be profound, augmenting and enhancing workers while transforming work. Jobs will be created, and other jobs will be destroyed, although even the jobs that are crippled by robotification will require new skills to flourish. As straightforward, simple, repetitive and mundane tasks are automated away, the aggregate demand for skills complementary and supportive of superhuman capabilities will increase.

Demand for advanced jobs will rise in areas such as artificial intelligence programming, bioengineering and neural interface design. At the same time, enjoyment of work will depend more heavily upon creativity, EQ and complex problem-solving – all things that humans are better at than machines.

To prepare for these changes, employers and policymakers need to invest in their existing workforce. This means prioritising things like reskilling and upskilling programmes at work, increasing support for enriching STEM (science, technology, engineering, and mathematics) education at school, and funding for employees to continue learning as they transition to new roles. It also means creating more opportunities for new kinds of learning cultures and competitions at work – pitting teams of employees against one another to see who can come up with the best suspension design, the best formula for a jet engine, or the best recipe for ice-cream. In this way, society can ensure that individuals and organisations remain adaptable and able to thrive in a superhuman world.

7

Superhumans in Governance and Leadership

Augmented Leaders: Enhancing Decision-Making

With enhanced capabilities, we could reinvent governance and leadership. An augmented leader, for instance, could benefit from improved networks, richer data, brain-computer interface (BCI)-aided elimination of irrelevant information and near-real-time access to large, complicated datasets; therefore, such a leader will likely be better able to make sound decisions.

Better leaders could use AI for scenario modelling, predictive dynamics, understanding the effects of policy, spotting patterns in society and finding optimal solutions to current problems. For instance, leaders might employ AI to predict economic shifts before they become apparent, to manage epidemics better, mitigate pandemics or to address climate change and its consequences.

Using AI to foster better and more informed decision-making can help to remove bias and enhance the fairness and objectivity in policymaking.

But we are also troubled using augmentation in leadership: ethical considerations must be built in from the start. Some key questions arise, for instance: how can such systems be deployed in appropriately responsible ways? How can their decision-making processes be rendered accountable and open? What kinds of safeguards can be established to make sure that they are not being misemployed – for instance, biased data, or erosion of the individual as a political entity? How will augmentation of leadership shape the divide between those who are governed and those who govern – will it simply make leaders better able to serve their communities more effectively?

Governance Models for a Superhuman Society

The blending of superhuman potential into our collective lives also requires we reflect upon the composition of our institutions and how they govern. Hierarchical approaches to governance may need to yield to more collaborative, participatory approaches that capture augmented capacities across whole groups of people.

Just as governance could become more distributed in a superhuman society, but more hands-on, for example, with empowered individuals taking direct responsibility for decision-making at all functional levels, so the advent of new technologies, such as blockchain and distributed ledger systems, could enable truly transparent and accountable governance that empowers the citizens to direct and, importantly, to hold their leaders to account.

Furthermore, by utilising augmented reality (AR) and virtual reality (VR) technologies, we can provide better opportunities for citizens to physically 'show up' for public dialogue and deliberation around public policy issues. This would allow citizens to 'show up' in new and meaningful ways while also mitigating geographic and social divides between citizens.

Public Policy:
Shaping the Future

Public policy will play a key role in ensuring that superhuman technologies deliver these benefits, while also mitigating their risks. Policies towards innovation and augmentation must strike a balance between fostering new technologies and guarding against unethical or socially damaging outcomes.

Policies should also promote more equitable access to enhancement technologies so that all people regardless of socioeconomic status can benefit. These include subsidising basic enhancements, support for public awareness and education, as well as inclusive innovation ecosystems.

Aside from all those potential scientific, technological and economic difficulties, however, policymakers will need to tackle the ethical and social issues raised by the applications of superhuman technologies. What rules are appropriate to ensure that emerging technologies such as genetic engineering and neural interfaces, and the development of artificial superhuman intelligence (ASI), are applied responsibly and for the greater good? How can we protect individual freedoms and autonomy, and privacy, when superhuman technologies are developed and deployed? Such questions will have to be addressed on the international level, with a view to developing the foundations of global standards and regimes that will guarantee the safe and equitable deployment of a range of superhuman technologies.

With ethical norms that recognise and promote fairness, equality and other commonly valued individual and social goods embedded in public policy, a world of superhumans might be one where we want to live.

8

Cultural and Psychological Impacts

Redefining Identity:
Psychological Effects of Augmentation

This shift will have more subtle but powerful implications for how we see ourselves and others. When brain or body upgrades become an integral part of a meaningful sense of self, questions arise regarding what it means to be human. These effects can be profound and psychologically impactful.

With improvements in brainpower, muscle mass and sensory perception come increases in feelings of empowerment and self-efficacy (the belief that we can do things). But these empowerments in turn create tensions around questions of identity and authenticity: what aspects of these abilities are 'ours' and which come through technological amplification?

Secondly, enhanced augmentees might be seen by the un-augmented as somehow incomplete or lacking in some way, perhaps leading to feelings of inadequacy, envy or social exclusion on the part of the non-augmented. To guard against these possibilities, we need a culture that encourages a wide variety of human expressions and achievements, and that fully acknowledges human achievement on many paths to personal and societal completeness.

Cultural Shifts: Embracing New Norms

As human-centred technologies increasingly become more superhuman, cultural norms and values inevitably need to change; societies need to adjust their rules for living, working and socialising to reflect these new technologies. This has implications for everything from the arts to ethics.

For example, in the arts, superhuman capacities might inspire new styles of artistic expression that extend human creativity into technological innovation. Improvements in augmented and virtual reality portals can produce experiences whose format demands a re-imagining of storytelling, performance and visual art. A similar logic can be applied to other enhancements to cognitive and sensory capacities.

From an ethical standpoint, societies will have to decide what augmentation means for notions of fairness, merit and equality. The cultural acceptance of superhuman technology will depend on whether these advances are congruent with social norms and values, and whether they are viewed as accessible and inclusive.

Addressing Resistance:
Overcoming Fear and Misinformation

These superhuman blood technologies are inevitably going to meet resistance in the form of fear of the unknown and considerations of safety, ethics and misinformation. This resistance needs to be arrested by educating the masses, acting transparently and having discussions.

Public education efforts can demystify superhuman technologies, by providing clear explanations of their benefits and risks and refuting common myths and misunderstandings. By arming the public with accurate information, the chances of public rejection of socially beneficial technology can be decreased.

Superhuman systems must also be transparent in their development and use. Making research, funding and regulatory processes open and accountable can dampen fears that they will be misused or have unforeseen outcomes. Societal engagement with the much needed, if sometimes contentious, would-be debaters (ethicists and sociologists, among others) can help in this regard as well. Most of all, though, the people who might be affected have a right to be heard.

In addition, empathic cultures will surely cultivate an environment where augmented and un-augmented analogues can coexist – not least because the key ideals underlying the ideal of human flourishing are by no means exclusive. The chief claims made on our allegiance by any given conception will not fundamentally clash with such ideals. This means that societies can maintain their cohesion despite the new cultural and psychological dynamics of the super humanist era.

9

Ensuring Safety and Security

Protecting Against Cyber Threats: The New Frontier

Such super-technologies will even be ingrained in our bodies and minds, and properly securing those technologies is essential as the augmented human being is also interacting with networks and embedded devices via neural interfaces and other upgrades. This raises the potential of new cyber threats to beat back that cybersecurity and cause harm. Proper risk auditing is vital.

Security features, such as encryption, authentication, and intrusion detection mechanisms, must be built into neural interfaces, as well as other forms of augmentation, from the start. A monitoring process for tracking and responding to new vulnerabilities must be put into place and updated over time. Such technologies should also be accompanied by programmes to educate users about best practices and risks related to safety.

The stakes are especially high for superhuman players who directly influence society, such as military personnel, medical personnel and government officials. Secure superhuman systems can help preserve public safety and security and instil confidence in the public. International co-operation and information-sharing can also be crucial components of cybersecurity, since superhuman technologies often work in networks whose security is relevant globally. If something is a risk in one system, it is likely a risk in every other system.

Safeguarding Personal Data: Privacy in a Superhuman World

Another issue raised by the emergence of superhuman technologies is privacy and the protection of personal data. Neural interfaces, genetic enhancements and other augmentations can generate vast amounts of personal data, with health-related information, patterns of cognitive functioning and insights into behavioural patterns within its remit.

Such regulatory frameworks must provide a clear directive about how information can be collected and stored, with no surprises for people in terms of where their data is held – and who has access to it. Certainly, it is important to develop and maintain appropriate protocols for consent, so that people can specify who gets access to what information and for what purpose. It may also be necessary to utilise anonymisation and/or cryptography protocols to ensure that identifiable personal information is not rendered open to unauthorised access.

Besides this, corporations developing and deploying superhuman technologies must conduct their business in accordance with ethical data practices. This includes enhancing user privacy and transparency by performing regular audits of potential vulnerabilities, engaging the open review of stakeholders and the establishment of successful transparency by checking that concerns are appropriately heard.

Establishing International Security Standards

Since superhuman technologies are global in character, it will be necessary to develop international security protocols for their application to ensure that they are used in a safe and humane manner. There are opportunities for governments, business, and international organisations to work together to create a common resource to respond to augmentation ever more effectively.

Good international standards can codify the development, use and oversight of superhuman technologies, facilitating comparability and compatibility across jurisdictions, while encouraging sharing of information and cooperation on issues such as cyber defences, personal-data protection and ethical use.

If we create a comprehensive global framework towards the safe and sane use of superhumans – a framework based on openness and sharing, and with the wellbeing of our entire species at its core – there is hope that we can surpass present concerns and leverage these technologies toward a future that benefits us all.

10

Innovation and Entrepreneurship

Fostering Innovation:
The Role of Superhumans in Startups

This is leading to new kinds of opportunities for innovation, start-ups and entrepreneurialism. This not only includes people using AR and VR to escape the struggles of the real world, but also new superhuman individuals who can think faster, see more, hear more, and react quicker than previously possible. These kinds of people can develop new tech, products, services and solutions like never before.

Superhumans or superhuman entrepreneurs would be able to leverage their enhanced mental functionalities to spot emerging trends, identify hidden problems and devise innovative solutions earlier and quicker than ever before. AI-powered tools and neural interfaces can help unleash creativity and strategic thinking and force entrepreneurs to discover new business models and technologies that could foil existing business models.

The entrepreneurial ecosystem should support and foster super-human innovators by providing them with funding and resources and by creating incubators and accelerators programmed for su-perhuman technologies; they could encourage superhuman en-trepreneurs to confront one another and co-work and could keep them in touch with tech moguls and investors.

Case Studies:
Successful Superhuman-Driven Ventures

Several first-emission startups and ventures have already shown the way toward superhuman technologies. Though anecdotal, these case studies indicate that augmentation can indeed catalyse innovation and entrepreneurship.

For instance, Elon Musk's company, Neuralink – a company devising brain-computer interfaces of the highest complexi-ty – is working on devices that can effectively read and write our thoughts. Neuralink's technology, as it's currently being described, will have the ability to boost brainpower and break down barriers between human and machine. By providing direct access to control AI as well as other digital systems, Neuralink opens the door for novel forms of medical treatment, education and communication.

Another is OpenAI, a research centre whose mission is to 'pro-mote the development of safe artificial general intelligence and ensure that its economic benefits are widely distributed'. Some of the work done at OpenAI, such as developing relatively general-purpose AI systems that also integrate with human cognition, could lead to more efficient decision-making, creativity and innovation in many areas.

These ventures suggest that superhuman technologies will incentivise innovation, create new market opportunities, and help address some of the most urgent global problems.

Future Trends: Where Innovation is Headed

Superhuman technologies are the future of innovation and entrepreneurship, and I suggest we will see several trends going forward as those technologies proliferate.

Firstly, AI, biotech and neural interfaces will create personalised products and services on steroids. Medical treatments, educational travel experiences, consumer goods – all will be skewed dramatically towards a culture of personalisation driven by superhuman innovators.

Second, AR and VR (augmented reality and virtual reality) will bring more people online and give them the chance to engage in immersive interactions. These technologies will make in-person experiences more engaging by bringing more digital content into the real world or changing the environment in a way that entices you to explore and use that content. AR and VR could similarly transform how people engage with entertainment, education and retail.

Third, shifting priorities towards sustainability and social impact will spur innovation in areas such as clean energy, environmental conservation and social equity. Superhuman entrepreneurs will lead the development of solutions for the world's current and future challenges, helping to shape a brighter and more inclusive future for humanity.

Advance mining of these trends is a crucial element of what we've dubbed the 'science of technology futures', which arms near-future innovators, entrepreneurs and visionaries with tools to create what we call 'superhuman' or super-intelligent products, services and solutions – the human behaviours of tomorrow whose robustness are built in the laboratory and potential accelerated through the real-world crucible.

11

Building a Resilient Society

Community Resilience:
Preparing for Technological Disruptions

Especially as super-technologies become increasingly embedded into society, it's important to lay foundations of community resilience, in case technological structures make disruptions more possible, or more difficult to navigate. Technologies can create new opportunities but can also lead to new uncertainties – and communities need to be able to cope.

Adaptive resilience would create the opportunity for everyone to develop the ability to use technological change to flourish within an ever-changing world so that his community remains strong and tight knit. Social networks could broaden and deepen, communities could work to become inclusive, and members could be encouraged to become more active in all kinds of decision-making. If members of the village community were invited to contribute to discussions about superhuman technology deployment and its uses, effects and implications, they would become more resilient to the new world emerging as a result.

And finally, educational programmes can be catalysed to stoke social resilience. If people are well-versed in technological changes and have the skills, they need to take advantage of new opportunities and/or mitigate new risk factors, they may be more equipped to adapt to unforeseen forces. Lifelong learning programmes, community workshops, and public information campaigns could help usher in an era of technology-savvy societies where everyone is prepared for what might lie ahead.

Collaborative Approaches: Governments, Businesses, and Individuals

This is what is it is going to take to build a shared, democratic and resilient society world within which superhuman technologies, whatever they may eventually entail, can be harnessed to benefit everyone, rather than exploit those who cannot afford to have less-than-superhuman capabilities. Governments, companies and individuals, each of whom must perform a part, have a stake in achieving this.

Governments have the power to enact policies and regulations to balance access to enhancement technologies and increase individual rights protections without excessively hindering innovation – so long as they also invest in the public education and infrastructure essential for a smoothly functioning community in the age of superhumans.

Businesses can incentivise the responsible development and deployment of superhuman technologies by encouraging innovation and economic growth, building ethical cultures, engaging with stakeholders, and promoting inclusive and respectful corporate cultures and democratic practices. Working alongside governments and communities is one way that businesses can shape the world in which they and everyone else can thrive.

Also, individuals can help to build resilience. Staying abreast of technological change, for example, talking about it, rather than avoiding it, can all help to create an informed society. People also need to develop their own personal resilience: the skills and flexibility to harness new technologies for their own benefit.

Vision for a Sustainable Superhuman Society

Superhuman projects should aim at making a better world accessible for all: a world that is ecologically sustainable and no longer inequitable. This will require commitment to justice, equity and environmental sustainability.

The main goal for a sustainable superhuman society is for humanity to become better, promoting an even socially distributed, empowering, diverse and inclusive, and rights-based society. To create this relationship with the next generation of technologies, superhuman enhancements must benefit everyone by redressing social inequalities and embracing diversity and inclusion.

Moreover, it's important to embed the precautionary principle as a necessary condition for pioneering and adopting superhuman entities. Contrary to the fear depicted in techno-dystopian narratives, the actualisation of our technological destiny does not have to mean a loss of humanity. In fact, such a transformation would not only enrich humanity's existence but also pave the way for a new and elevated kind of human experience.

Environmental sustainability is another crucial aspect of the vision. Superhuman technologies might facilitate innovations in clean energy and resource use, as well as focusing more targeted efforts in environmental conservation. In this way, we can temper the current warming of the planet and slow current trends in biodiversity loss. By using such technologies responsibly, we have within our grasp the ability to make our place in this world more sustainable.

This will require ongoing dialogue and collaboration for all those involved – we are after all in this together. In this way, society can bypass the current Phase Space, leapfrog the 'superhuman bottleneck', and plan for a post-singularity future in which future generations of superhumans have the greatest likelihood of thriving – individually, and collectively.

12

Preparing for the Transition

Individual Preparedness: Steps to Take Today

Once we have concluded that a superhuman future is likely to be crafted by those companies and governments that are sufficiently in control of their technological trajectory to control their super humanisation, the question of the role of the individual becomes critical. What every citizen should be doing now is gearing up to take maximum advantage of and best cope with the challenges that will arise from a superhuman future.

What is the first step you can take? Inform yourself about the cutting edge of the superhuman technologies that are brewing, about the benefits and risks, as well as the moral and sociopolitical consequences of these instruments. By doing so, you will be in a better position to decide both how you want to engage with these tools – if you should engage at all – and how you can advocate for their responsible use.

Investing in education and developing human skill is also well-advised. As new types of skills and knowledges become necessary, we should aim to acquire new and further education and further develop our professional skills. Such future learning opportunities encompass education in AI, biotech, etc, as well as skills in critical and creative thinking and adaptability.

Aspect two of individual preparedness is building a supportive community. Connecting with other people who are transhumanist and interested in high-tech superhumanity can be a great resource for insights, support and resources. Such a community could include professional societies, conferences and workshops, and online communities.

Community Initiatives: Building Local Resilience

In this way, communities can play a key role in preparing for the transition to the superhuman era. Local initiatives can cultivate resiliency and ensure that all members of the community can thrive in the new world of technological determinism.

Even so, community education programmes can raise awareness about superhuman technologies and their repercussions. Providing materials, resources, and information that is easy to access can help people learn about the advantages and pitfalls of enhancements and prepare them for decisions they may someday face. Workshops, seminars, and public forums can also help people to talk about their concerns related to superhuman technologies and their implications. Such programmes help community members to grapple with the moral enigmas of emerging technologies while using rational discourse, rather than remaining silent and allowing others to dictate their realities.

Local levels of government and civil society can do likewise, by investing in infrastructure and resources for resilience, such as building public buildings that promote learning and collaboration (libraries, community centres, maker spaces) and investing in technology and digital literacy programmes that usher in everyone into a superhuman society.

Collaborative efforts that build on partnerships between diverse stakeholders can help build resilience in communities. For instance, bringing together local businesses, schools and community organisations builds an enabling ecosystem for innovation, inclusivity and sustainability.

Global Collaboration: Working Together for a Better Future

The move towards the superhuman future is a global challenge to which there simply is no individual answer. To get this right, the world needs to work together to create global standards and frameworks that will guide the development and deployment of superhuman technologies in a safe and beneficial way.

International organisations or coalitions can help foster collaboration and dialogue in this regard. Bringing together experts, policymakers and stakeholders from around the world to discuss the values, needs, and concerns surrounding superhuman technologies can help with ensuring that sensible deliberations take place. Sharing knowledge and best practices among nations can lead to more coordinated strategies in how to use this technology to address global challenges on the one hand, and to ensure more equal access to enhancements on the other.

International collaboration can also support research and innovation globally. Closer international cooperation can help us overcome development barriers to superhuman technologies more quickly and in ways that will benefit all human beings. This can include international commitments and investments in research with broad global goals, such as health, sustainability and social equity.

In addition, international cooperation is needed to provide security and to ensure civil liberties for superhumans. Consistent cross-border standards for cybersecurity and data protection can ensure that enhancements are used in a way that protects the integrity of personal data.

Conclusion:
Embracing the Future

The growing threat of superhuman technologies will bring new opportunities and challenges as a tsunami of disruptive technologies change the fabric of society. Before that day comes, however, we can begin preparing for the inevitable by training ourselves, our communities and our nations to take advantage of the opportunities – while mitigating the potentially dire risks and ethical dilemmas that might come with these superhuman technologies.

To move forward, we must adopt a lifelong mindset of openness to learning, cooperation, and inclusion. By opening ourselves to empathy and supportive ways of communicating, we can create a world where human-sped technologies are embraced, where Robo Paralympians are enthusiastically received, and where smooth collaboration leads the way. With advance planning and international cooperation, we can create a future for enhanced humans and for society.

13

Conclusion:
Charting a Course for a Superhuman Future

Towards the dawn of the Superhuman Era, the melding of bespoke human-machine systems is set to transform our world in unprecedented ways. This book has endeavoured to delve deep into the many dimensions of this shift, from the emergence of new human capacities, capabilities and behaviours that will come in the wake of technology-fuelled transhumanism, to the questions of ethics, manageability, and governance that will follow on from the very possibilities it will afford. It ends here, with a call to synthesise and chart the way forward for the Superhuman Age.

Embracing the Opportunities

Superhuman technologies will create unprecedented opportunities for enhancing the human condition, ambitiously – but appropriately – seeking to solve some of the shiniest and sharpest problems of our age. We can expand access to health. We can democratise education. We can accelerate economic growth and promote social equity.

But superhuman technologies can transform healthcare too, including diagnostics, treatment and prevention. Consider AI-powered diagnostic tools, enabling clinicians to make more informed diagnoses; personalised medicine, facilitated by genetic engineering; or neural interfaces, providing hope for the treatment of neurologic disorders. Each of these innovations has the potential to decrease healthcare expenditures, improve health outcomes and make state-of-the-art medical care more accessible to all.

In education, similar cognitive enhancements and AI-supported learning could herald a new era of personalised and efficient education. Students would be able to learn at their own rate, taking advantage of specially tailored curricula that embrace their own unique strengths and weaknesses. We would hopefully raise a generation of learners better equipped to take on the problems of the future.

Economically, a proliferation of superhumans could boost creativity, create new industries and accelerate growth. Superhumans, with intellect and speed far greater than ours and physical reflexes five times faster than a Spaniard, could fuel entrepreneurship and technological innovation, creating products and services that we can, at best, only partially imagine today.

Socially, enhancements could be a way to bridge divides and

create more inclusion. Superhuman technologies hold the potential to benefit disabled and other marginalised groups, reduce inequalities, and provide a more equal society. This cannot be taken for granted, however. It will require proactive steps to prevent access from widening divides and to promote inclusion.

Addressing the Challenges

The opportunities are huge, but so are the challenges. Ethics, morals and social thought need to play a hand in developing and using superhuman technologies so they can benefit all humans.

Ethically, there are questions about human identity and where to draw the line between therapy and enhancement. If we can make ourselves physically fitter and smarter, what does it mean to be human, and where should we draw the line between therapy and enhancement? Regulatory regimes must also be put in place, to ensure that we use safe and effective enhancements in the right ways.

Socially, there are also fears about the creation of new forms of social stratification and separation. Supertech could lead to a new social split between have version of cases and have-not version. A policy response to this serious issue would include ways of making key enhancements access for all through subsidisation, for example, as well as for research and development to be funded in the public sphere.

This task will involve a cultural shift in norms and values. Communities will have to adapt to new patterns of living, working and interacting. They must incorporate the diversity of how people might choose to interact within their customs of inclusivity and respect.

Preparing for the Transition

That's why we must be prepared for a superhuman future, and why each of us has to do our part. That means being more deliberate about what we're doing – how we're raising our families, building our communities and countries, and how we're taking care of our planet – because the real work lies ahead.

People can prepare by keeping abreast of the latest superhuman technologies, acquiring skills and building networks, engaging in lifelong learning and openness to change, adapting to continuous technological change.

Communities can cultivate resilience through local programmes that encourage education, inclusivity, pluralism, deliberation and the organic formation of new social groups. For example, think about ways to enable local conversations regarding the implications of superhuman technologies. Engage citizens in town halls, readings, writing- and discussion groups. Encourage citizens to consider the impact of advanced technologies on their core social values. Local governments and local organisations can fund infrastructure and resources that support resilience; build technology capacity and foster greater access to digital literacy programmes.

Action at the level of international cooperation and collaboration is needed – standards and frameworks for the responsible development and deployment of superhuman technologies must be developed and agreed upon at a global scale. The security and privacy ramifications of various technologies must be addressed equally for all nations involved, and research and innovation must be conducted ethically, and yield results aimed at benefitting all of humanity.

A Call to Action

The superhuman future is coming for us – now is the moment to direct the superhuman future wisely, responsibly, and in the interests of humanity. This book has laid out the ways in which the superhuman future can go right, and the ways it can go wrong. And now it is your turn.

We must embrace these developments as an opportunity, while addressing where they go wrong with eyes wide open about what they will bring. That means governments, businesses and individuals, and communities working together. If we do, then their rise will bring an equitable, inclusive and prosperous humankind.

Imagine a future world of transhuman technologies that increases human ability, prosperity and the possibilities for an improved, more sustainable world, as well as increases wellbeing for enhanced humans and society at large. This is not pure fantasy – we can make it happen, if we choose to do so, act upon it, and care about the ethics and social justice that would make this possible.

Final Thoughts

A merging with superhuman technologies marks one of the biggest shifts in human history, and it's possible that it will be our final leap forward or the beginning of an uncharted human future. How we cope with it will depend not only on the facts we glean, but also on our willingness to embrace a culture defined by greater curiosity, creativity – and responsibility.

This book has served as a survival guide for the superhuman future, providing both a roadmap for seizing its opportunities and a toolbox for avoiding its dangers. The future never 'just happens'; it is something we shape for ourselves, every moment of every day.

Let's face those challenges together and begin sketching a path towards a more radically human world in which human potential continues to be maximised, humans accept greater diversity and cultivate more rounded, altruistic and inclusive societies. In a superhuman age, that is the world we're fighting for, and the struggle to reach it starts here and now. Let's get going.

PART II

Answers To 25 Frequently Asked Questions

(1). Superhuman Era: Preparing for the Future of Human Evolution

1.1. Embracing Cognitive Enhancements

Ultimately, we will step into a cognitive enhancement era. Accordingly, this era of transhumanism will see massive changes to how we learn, work, communicate and interact with others. Just think about how neural implants and other technologies such as brain-machine interface, designed to interact with an artificial intelligence (AI), can enhance the speed of learning, enhance memories and lead to better creativity. The adoption of these new technologies in the classroom can greatly improve education by personalising learning experiences based on individual learning styles, abilities and needs. Similarly, in the workplace, the use of cognitive enhancement can lead to better productivity, by accelerating the pace of thought and problem-solving, thus leading to faster innovation. While the rewards of cognitive enhancement can't be ignored, the massive adoption of this norm is not without several ethical and societal considerations such as equity, access and the likelihood of cognitive divide.

1.2. Physical Augmentation through Technology

Physical augmentation using biotechnology and robotics advancements will allow humans to go faster, jump higher and feel more. Exoskeletons to augment strength and endurance, neuro-prosthetics to give control over body movements, genetic enhancements to help prevent disease and increase physical abilities are just the tip of the iceberg. We'll want to understand ethical and regulatory frameworks to ensure the safety, accessibility and appropriate use of these technologies, particularly if they are used to help people with disabilities lead more independent lives. These technologies will bring tremendous benefits.

1.3. Genetic Engineering and the Superhuman Future

Genetic engineering fuelled by CRISPR and other forms of gene-editing stands to eradicate genetic diseases, enhance physical and cognitive traits and extend the healthy human lifespan. The capacity to alter the human genome with pinpoint precision would foster a new era of human evolution. However, this power will carry not only extraordinary promise but also profound potential for harm and controversy – from the possibility of 'off-target' effects, to the potential for creating an underclass. If our superhuman destiny ever becomes a reality, we will want to have robust regulatory regimes and ethical guidelines in place to guide its use.

1.4. Ethical and Social Implications of Human Enhancement

The move to the human+ age is filled with ethical and social perils. Human enhancements available only to a select few could further entrench social inequalities, creating a bifurcated society of enhanced and non-enhanced humans. The very process of seeking to achieve perfection through human enhancement raises fundamental questions about identity, diversity and what it means to be human. Policymakers, ethicists and technologists must work together to develop policies that are inclusive and ensure broad and equitable access to enhancements while also sharing the benefits of emerging technology across society.

1.5. Redefining Human Potential

Possibility – as we enhance ourselves physically, cognitively, and socially using cutting-edge technologies. And we're not just playing with potential metaphysical ideas. We might be ushering into existence a biologically based superhuman species. Our path out of this uncertain interphase is not yet clear. But if the future developments of accelerated human evolution deregulate our society, we need to start working on understanding, accepting, and preparing for the changes the superhuman era will bring. Perhaps it's not too late to hold a productive conversation among scientists, ethicists, policymakers, and members of the public about humanity's future trajectory. If we tackle the challenges thoughtfully and as a community, we can embrace the superhuman era's potential for an inclusive, ethical, and humane future for humanity.

(2) Beyond Humanity: Navigating the Rise of Super-humans

2.1. Superhuman Integration in Society

After the emergence of superhumans: It is essential how enhanced people are integrated into our society once we surpass thresholds of human capabilities. Excessive physical skills and intellectual capacity mean that some level of inequality between enhanced or unenhanced human beings is inevitable. It is also essential that we deliver policies and frameworks that enable us to coexist with enhanced people in a harmonious fashion. This means that policy must provide equitable possibilities for all to access any kind of enhancement at hand. Enhancing the general knowledge among people via public education and awareness campaigns will also help society to understand the emergence of the superhuman and endorse the development of the super-coherent society.

2.2. Legal and Regulatory Considerations

The creation of superhumans will require adjustments in legal and regulatory frameworks. For example, privacy and consent frameworks will need to be rethought to reflect new abilities, and intellectual property rights will need to consider new ways of working that may be enabled by superhuman capacities. Work is needed to establish legal frameworks around such conceptual 'grey areas', ensuring everyone gets a fair share of the benefits of superhuman capabilities, and ensuring these benefit society without overstepping individual rights. This will require the cooperation of governments and international bodies.

2.3. Ethical Dilemmas in Human Enhancement

Human enhancement technologies present significant ethical quandaries. The possibility of improving physical and cognitive abilities carries with it the potential emergence of a new kind of inequality, in which enhanced humans possess tremendous advantages over humans who have not been enhanced. To prevent the worst human enhancement technologies from being developed and deployed in ways that further harm, we must make sure that ethical considerations guide every step of the process. Expert ethicists, scientists, politicians and policymakers, and the public at large should debate the ethical parameters of human enhancement.

2.4. Economic Impact of Superhuman Capabilities

The rise of superhumans would have profound economic consequences, too. Indeed, superhuman individuals could lead to innovation and productivity growth through an acceleration in human capital formation and technological innovations. They could also lead to economic growth. Yet, such polymorphs might cause job displacements or economic losses by emptying the market of specialised jobs or leading to polarisation of occupations, with the growth of white-collar professional services jobs at one end of the spectrum and low-end service jobs and misemployment at the other end. Policies to stimulate productivity and economic growth would need to go together with policies to mitigate these negative effects such as support for workforce transition, re-training programmes and measures to ensure the rising tide of superhuman steadily lifts all boats.

2.5. Global Cooperation for Superhuman Advancements

Global cooperation will be essential in preventing a superhuman divide from driving nations apart. Open scientific collaboration shared ethical guidelines, and universal distribution of enhancement technologies would help nations share in humanity's precarious transition. International cooperation would also help us address potential threats, namely the wanton misuse of superhuman technologies for military or coercive power. These questions admire the value of international collaboration, whether in scientific research, regulatory oversight or foreign policy. But how feasible is global cooperation in practice, especially when nations' real interests are at odds? Arms control is instructive: while no system is foolproof, individual countries benefit from broad-based agreements as evidenced by the successful 1987 Intermediate-Range Nuclear Forces Treaty and most other nuclear weapons agreements. Similar commitments by the world's leading powers to forgo bio-enhancements that confer military advantage could also aid national security.

(3) Superhumans vs. Humans: Embracing the Next Frontier

3.1. Balancing Human and Superhuman Interests

As we move closer to a superhuman future, making enhancements available to everyone in such a way as to better balance the interests of enhanced and non-enhanced citizens will become vital. Enhancements can provide substantial benefits, from improving job prospects, earning potential and academic performance, to playing sports or socialising. Obviously, we need to embrace and celebrate a diversity of interests and goals, and policies must be enacted that maximise equal access to enhancements and the wellbeing of present and future generations, while minimising the possibility of particular benefits becoming confined to a narrow range of citizens. Meaningful discourse and cooperation between different sectors of the public can help to ensure that all of us benefit from the emerging superhuman state of humanity.

3.2. The Role of Education in a Superhuman Society

Schools and Universities will have to learn to cater for Superhumans, the kind of cognitive enhancement we envisage will require novel modes of learning and teaching and will enhance the potential of personalised education. There will be a need for some form of cross-fertilisation of educational approaches in which educationalists will have to be innovative to provide adaptive learning environments that are suitable for the diversity of learner needs, particularly when individuals continue learning throughout their lifetime. More importantly, we believe that in addition to academic materials, ethical education will have to become an integral part of the curriculum to prepare many generations to come for living in a superhuman society and to cultivate empathy and understanding for those who are not cognitively enhanced.

3.3. Psychological Impacts of Human Enhancement

The psychological implications of human enhancement are complicated and multilayered. Enhanced individuals might face identity issues, and societal pressure, while non-enhanced individuals might struggle with a sense of inadequacy or exclusion. Resilience and intervention systems need to evolve to provide support within these new social dynamics, by facilitating access to tailored services to enhance wellbeing and eudaimonia – evolutionary wellbeing. Support for mental health education among both enhanced and non-enhanced individuals can help build an environment that mitigates the psychosocial effects of human enhancement.

3.4. Ethics of Enhancement: Ensuring Fairness and Safety

As we enter the new era of human enhancement, ethical considerations must take centre stage. We have a responsibility to make enhancements as safe and effective as possible, and to ensure widespread implementation across all segments of society where governmental regulations or other social constraints have marked inequality. Importantly, we should take steps to ensure that technologies to enhance humans are harnessed for the betterment of humanity, and that the unintended consequences of technological advancements are given appropriate consideration. A number of ethical voices and leaders are engaged in these critical conversations. We need to listen to them.

3.5. Fostering Empathy and Inclusivity

Encouraging empathy and cooperation between enhanced and non-enhanced individuals will be essential to ensuring a cosmopolitan and harmonious society. A good education programme, supported by a strong range of social schemes and policies, that boosts empathy, emotional intelligence and cultural sensitivity can help build bridges between the enhanced and the non-enhanced. We should strive to ensure that tomorrow's society is one where all are welcome, whatever their enhancement capabilities.

(4) The Superhuman Frontier: Opportunities and Dangers Ahead

4.1. Harnessing Superhuman Abilities for Good

The possibility of superhuman enhancements gives hope to many of our biggest global challenges and to improving living quality for most people today. Wider cognitive and physical capabilities can promote innovation that leads to better healthcare, environmental sustainability and space exploration. We can utilise those superhuman enhancements for the common good to solve the biggest problems of our time – climate change, disease and resource scarcity. So, we need an intelligent and ethical policy for superhuman enhancements that sets them to work for the benefit of all of us.

4.2. Risks of Unregulated Human Enhancement

This lack of control could be extremely dangerous if left unregulated and could lead to unexpected consequences for individuals who might use these enhancements, such as health problems, or more general issues like the growth of social inequality, if certain enhancements become available only to those with high incomes. Uncontrolled use of genetic engineering and AI could breed new ethical minefields – for instance, one party accessing enhancements that others believe are dangerous. To prevent these dangers, it would be necessary to develop thorough regulatory frameworks that would assure the safety of enhancements, their effectiveness, and the responsible use of those enhancements.

Governments, aided by international bodies, and eventually aided by the scientific community itself (including ethicists), would have a key role to play in drawing up the guidelines that would govern the use of human enhancement.

4.3. Medical Innovations and Superhuman Healthcare

Superhuman medical breakthroughs will lead the way. As regenerative medicine, prostheses and gene therapies proliferate, they will subject superhuman bodies to new treatments, and turn cure and prevention into new possibilities. Wider dissemination of medical superhumanity would require new medical protocols, specialised therapies and therapists trained in the idiosyncrasies of the superhuman condition. The challenge will be learning how to make the innovations available equitably and ethically.

4.4. Preparing for Technological Disruptions

Technological disruptions are a given on the superhuman trajectory. A disruptive rate of innovation has the potential for social and economic disruption. The necessary preparation for this disruption could include broad and forward-looking social, economic and political planning. Of course, how best to instigate timely disruption depends on many factors. An overall goal should necessarily be how best to identify or anticipate potential disruptive changes, and to prepare industries and communities for them. This could include aiding worker and industrial adjustment and transition through specific pathways such as retraining, reskilling, upskilling, lifelong learning, and state benefits. Undoubtedly, the superhuman landscape will involve a level of social and economic disruption along the way. In order to be successful, it is imperative that we anticipate it, educate ourselves for it, and cooperatively plan for it.

4.5. Public Perception and Acceptance

Perceptions will play a huge role – public understanding, clear communication, public education and carefully crafted policy will build trust and openness. Dealing with fear and false assumptions through open discussion and evidence.

There's a way in which information that emphasises a 'you-based' sense of disconnection from others can facilitate a more positive attitude towards superhuman enhancement. Promoting public discussion of the various intersecting ethical, social and economic issues raised by HETs can create a more informed (and therefore supportive) social climate for advancing human life and could lead to people finding ways of sharing an enchanted planet with human enhancement.

(5) Superhuman Revolution: A Guide to Thriving in the Age of Advanced Intelligence

5.1. Adapting to Cognitive Enhancements

In conjunction with giving rise to new ways of thinking, learning and working, the permanent integration of cognitive adjustments in the human condition would likely prove essential to individuals' and societies' successful navigation through the ever-changing landscape of cognitive enhancements, as well as the exponential increase in opportunities for enhanced memory, creativity and problem-solving that will ensue. Above all, the widespread use of cognitive-enhancing drugs and procedures seems likely to rekindle the flame of learning, and with it the pedagogical impetus for lifelong learning. In tune with the spirit of the times, educational institutions and procedures of various kinds would need to respond to the possibilities of personalised learning that would be created through the superhuman revolution.

5.2. Leveraging AI for Human Enhancement

This is the promise of the superhuman revolution, and bespoke AI plays an important role by providing a suite of tools and technologies that augment the capabilities of the human body and mind. AI can augment our healthcare, education and work prospects, with social-recommendation engines, bespoke learning platforms, intelligent assistants and augmented reality (AR). Though enhancing ourselves with AI will require more deliberation, the sheer ingenuity of machine learning, together with its transparency, auditability and capacity to provide digital bread-crumb trails, will hopefully allow us to strike the right balance between human augmentation and human degradation. All that is required is to ensure that AI technologies, products and devices are designed in such a way that we can use them optimally to our benefit, while minimising their risks and harms.

5.3. Navigating Ethical and Social Challenges

We face marked ethical and social problems in the age of the superhuman. If some enhancements are only available to the elites, it can lead to societal strata or divisions The development and deployment of enhancement technology should be guided by ethical policies and practices. Attention to human enhancement from different stakeholder groups could generate inclusive, equitable, fair and socially cohesive policies.

5.4. Building Resilience in a Superhuman World

If we are to flourish in the age of the superhuman, we need to be able to adapt. Technological change is transforming how we live, and each of us will be increasingly called upon to learn new ways of coping with change and uncertainty. These strategies will encompass developing mental and emotional resilience, learning new skills and forging new kinds of collaborations and networks. Creating a culture of adaptability will be essential to making the most of the opportunities emerging from the superhuman revolution.

5.5. Fostering Global Cooperation

Global cooperation is vital for shared research and ethical frameworks, and for widespread dissemination and for preventing a great haves-and-have-nots divide in the superhuman revolution. A shared framework on enhancement technologies would enable countries to work together toward different kinds of risks. Eternal life for a despot, for example, could make waging war more likely rather than less. Superintelligence could also be turned against the citizenry if technologies such as brain-machine interface and virtual-reality capsuling become tools of coercive control. Global agreements could assist countries in safeguarding against superhuman technologies being applied as military technologies. International agreements would be instrumental in spreading mutual benefits, maintaining peaceful relations among countries, and accelerating progress for the world.

Conclusion

The superhuman revolution holds out the promise of a radically transformative human civilisation – a future of superhumans, reinvigorating the idea of human evolution to continually push the thresholds of physical, cognitive and social human growth. In a world where technology is blending faster and faster into all aspects of our lives, we must also contend with the challenges and complexities that come along with our bravest endeavours thus far. If we are to address humanity's future evolution, it will deeply depend upon a great dialogue: scientists, ethicists, policymakers and the wider public must come together to discuss the challenges and opportunities of our superhuman future. If we can do so, and to create solutions together and with thoughtful preparation, we can utilise the superhuman era to create a future that is universally accessible, ethical and that ultimately improves the lives of all.

Significant References

1. Kurzweil, Ray. "The Singularity is Near: When Humans Transcend Biology" – This influential work by the futurist Ray Kurzweil proposes that a technological singularity (a transformative moment when artificial intelligence becomes smarter than humans) is inevitable, and that humanity might 'transcend biology' because of technology. Powerful because it synthesises the pessimistic views of RWA and Ray Norris and considers the potential implications for the reshaping of society.

2. Tegmark, Max. "Life 3.0: Being Human in the Age of Artificial Intelligence" – Max Tegmark, a world expert on quantum physics who is also known for his work on AI, examines the near future of our species, and what could happen when we create another life form: how can our species adapt and thrive in an age of artificial intelligence? He names his book Life 3.0 – In the near future, technological developments will allow us to create smarter-than-human intelligence. What happens then? Will AI enhance our lives or annex them? Could artificial intelligence perform a miracle and make humanity immortal? If so, should we view this as a incredibly positive development? Is it too good to be true? Where else would we want to go? To whom would we want to go there with? Will AI improve our lives or annex them? Will teachers, doctors and drivers be displaced by algorithms? Should we upgrade to be more like our machines? Should humans merge their brains with machines?

Will work be displaced? Brynjolfsson and McAfee – Is there a singularity at the end of the road for humans? Resnick – No one, not even the experts, has a clue about how work will change. Google's John Giannandrea – Our task is to help people and society citizens enhance their lives. Imagination cimpm, a human-AIAnalytics.net blogger – By 2030, more people will be employed in machine learning, robotics, artificial intelligence, and associated fields than in law, accounting, banking, and finance combined.

3. Bostrom, Nick. "Superintelligence: Paths, Dangers, Strategies" - The philosopher Nick Bostrom presents an overview of the various paths to superintelligence and the strategies needed for its safe development. His book is essential reading on the existential risk that superintelligence represents for humans and the ethical issues that are inseparable from its development.

4. Harari, Yuval Noah. "Homo Deus: A Brief History of Tomorrow" - Yuval Noah Harari's Homo Deus (2015) is a broad survey of what he says are inevitable future trajectories of human evolution, through a confluence of biotechnology and artificial intelligence. Incorporating science and technology studies, Harari projects what the ethical, philosophical and social implications might be when humans become like gods.

5. Elon Musk: Tesla, SpaceX, and the Quest for a Fantastic Future (2015) by Ashlee Vance - Ashlee Vance's authorised biography of Elon Musk surveys the inventor's quest to 'enhance human rights' via technological progress. Musk's companies include both Neuralink (pushing the limits of the brain) and SpaceX (pushing the limits of the sky), a concise summary of the future and how we get there. He and his moment are instructive, especially for how reinvented human methods might serve everyday lives.

6. Brynjolfsson, Erik, and McAfee, Andrew, The Second Machine Age: Work, Progress, and Prosperity in a Time of Brilliant Technologies - Brynjolfsson and McAfee are examining the economic and social effects of the digital revolution that now includes AI and automation. Their analysis of how these technologies is changing industries and labour markets is an essential backdrop to understanding the implications of making things superhuman.

7. Martin Ford, Rise of the Robots: Technology and the Threat of a Jobless Future – Martin Ford in Rise of the Robots (2015) talks about the coming economic upheaval enabled by automation and AI. In this book he discusses the massive employment disruptions that will be enabled by automation and AI, and the need for new economic and social policies to address the shift to 'the superhuman future'.

8. Schwab, Klaus. "The Fourth Industrial Revolution" - the rise of the Fourth Industrial Revolution [described as] the convergence of the physical, digital and biological worlds ... Fourth Industrial Revolution: How World Economic Forum is Redefining the Globalisation Paradigm (2016) by Klaus Schwab, founder of the World Economic Forum – This book helps situate superhuman technologies in larger conversations about technological change.

9. Russell, Stuart. "Human Compatible: Artificial Intelligence and the Problem of Control" - Stuart Russell, expert on AI, describes the problem of making AI systems that are compatible with human values and goals: How can we make future AI systems maximally beneficial and controllable? These are some of the hardest problems in AI but must be solved if humankind is to successfully navigate the risks inherent in developing superhuman technology.

10. Anderson, Chris. "Makers: The New Industrial Revolution" - Chris Anderson's book Makers (2012), which charts the rise of what is sometimes called the maker movement, and digital fabrication processes that enable 'desktop production', points to the growing potential to enhance mass creativity and innovation in the near and midterm future, through more humane, augmented bodies and enhanced cognitive and physical capabilities.

11. Pratchett, Terry, et al. "The Science of Discworld" - The plot of The Science of Discworld — which hit the shelves in 1999 as co-authored fiction in which science slips in alongside surreal fantasy — was not the main point. Never has imagining a radically enhanced humanity been approached with quite so much irreverent erudition.

12. Clark, Andy. "Natural-Born Cyborgs: Minds, Technologies, and the Future of Human Intelligence" - In his book Being There: Putting Brain, Body and World Together Again (2011), the philosopher Andy Clark labels this Manasa a Mapa, and argues that humans have always been cyborgs, as our minds are extended through our artefacts and technologies. This perspective helps to situate superhuman technologies along an evolutionary and cognitive enhancement continuum.

13. Chalmers, David. "The Conscious Mind: In Search of a Fundamental Theory" - Bridging the gap – between current and potential applications, and between philosophical theory and policy on the one hand, and the progress of research into neural interfaces and cognitive enhancement on the other – is difficult without a basic understanding of the philosophical issues at stake. Philosopher David Chalmers, whose writings focus on the mind-body problem and the general nature of consciousness, would be an ideal starting point for thinking harder about the implications of neural interfaces and cognitive enhancements for selfhood and human experience.

14. Chalmers, David. "Reality+: Virtual Worlds and the Problems of Philosophy" - In this book, Chalmers explores the philosophical implications of virtual reality and simulations. The questions he asks about possibility, reality and experience are important for considering the potential future of augmented and virtual reality in a superhuman society.

15. Kelly, Kevin. The Inevitable: Understanding the 12 Technological Forces That Will Shape Our Future - Kevin Kelly devised 'the 12 technologies of the next century' – they include artificial intelligence, augmented reality, and digital economics. His sunny vision and shrewd analysis offer a blueprint for understanding the forces transforming superhumanity.

16. Horvitz, Eric. "On the Horizon of AI: A Call for Action" - This seminal paper details the promise and pitfalls of AI, from its founder and current co-president, the distinguished researcher and longtime Microsoft employee Eric Horvitz, who urges responsible development and cooperation to help ensure that superhuman technologies are built right and deployed for good.

17. Thrun, Sebastian. "Artificial Intelligence and the Future of Humans" - Sebastian Thrun, pioneer of autonomous vehicles and AI, reflects on the consequences that AI will have on society and shares his views on the future of humans and AI: what will this collaboration bring? What obstacles are there for such a superhuman technology?

18. Lee, Kai-Fu. "AI Superpowers: China, Silicon Valley, and the New World Order" - The Edge author Kai-Fu Lee provides the most thorough investigation of AI globally with his analysis of the competition between the progress of China and the United States. He offers a crucial window on the geopolitical consequences of AI, as well as its transformation of the processes of innovation and employment on a global scale.

19. Wolfram, Stephen. "A New Kind of Science" - In his influential book A New Kind of Science (2002), Stephen Wolfram proposes an explanation of the nature of computing and complexity, serving as a theoretical basis for AI and the other technologies enabling super-humanity.

20. Lloyd, Seth. "Programming the Universe: A Quantum Computer Scientist Takes on the Cosmos" - Seth Lloyd's book blurs the boundary between quantum computing and cosmology the computational nature of the universe that sits at the core of his cosmological writings offers new perspectives on the future of computing and of 'human enhancement'.

If you have no idea where to turn for accessible material that provides a balanced and well-considered picture of the technological, ethical, social and philosophical challenges raised by the development and spread of superhuman technologies, these twenty references will provide a solid base.

SELECTED BOOKS PUBLISHED BY DR. SELVA

These books can be viewed/ bought by following the link below to the Amazon site:

https://selvasmail.com/selvasbooks

Alternatively, should you wish to view the books on your phone or tablet, you could scan the barcode below, which will also take you direct to the Amazon site.

BOOKS ON WELLNESS & HEALTH (7 BOOKS)

BOOKS ON ALZHEIMER'S DEMENTIA (6 BOOKS)

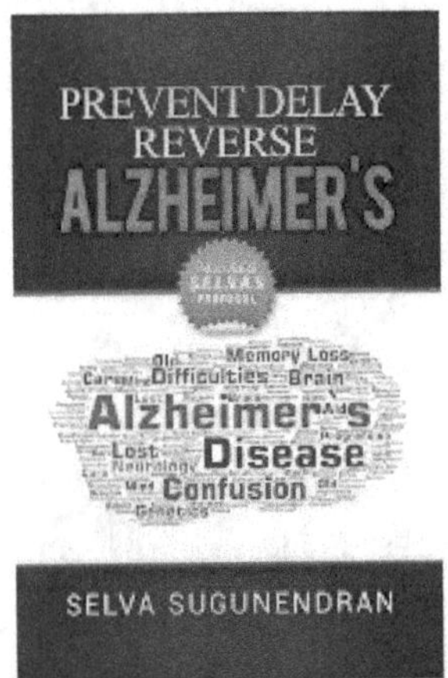

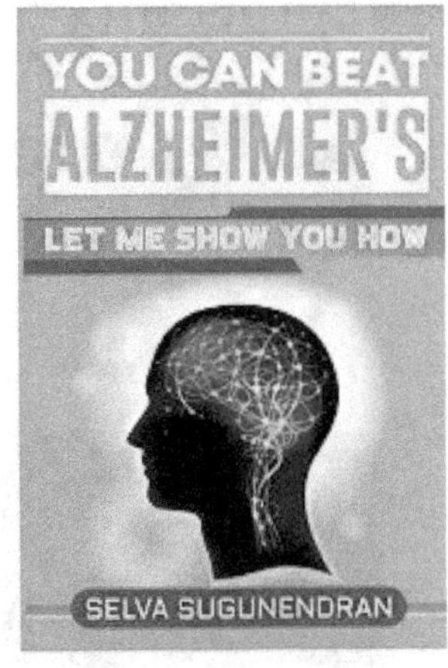

BOOKS ON SUCCESS (5 Books)

AI ROBOTICS (7 BOOKS)

AI and Its TRAJECTORY
Navigating the Age of Enlightenment and Addressing the Threats to Humanity
By DR. SELVA SUGUNENDRAN

SUPERHUMAN REVOLUTION
A Guide to Thriving in the Age of Advanced Intelligence
DR. Selva Sugunendran

AI TRILOGY:
NAVIGATING THE AI MAZE: ETHICS, CONTROL, AND INNOVATION
DR. SELVA SUGUNENDRAN

CHRISTIAN BOOKS (18 BOOKS)

THE IMPORTANCE OF
CHRISTIAN EDUCATION
FOR THE WELFARE OF CHILDREN
Christian Thought and Practice of Parenting and Educating Children
- About Church and God -
DR SELVA SUGUNENDRAN

PRAYER IS POWERFUL
ORGANISED CHRISTIAN PRAYERS TO ASK GOD FOR HELP FOR YOURSELF & YOUR LOVED ONES
SELVA SUGUNENDRAN

PATHWAYS OF LIGHT:
WALKING THE CHRISTIAN JOURNEY
DR. SELVA SUGUNENDRAN

A LIVE DEBATE
AMONGST 3 YOUNG SCIENTISTS
On Eight Key Areas of Evolution
SELVA SUGUNENDRAN

21 REASONS
Why Evolution Lacks Scientific Proof
SELVA SUGUNENDRAN

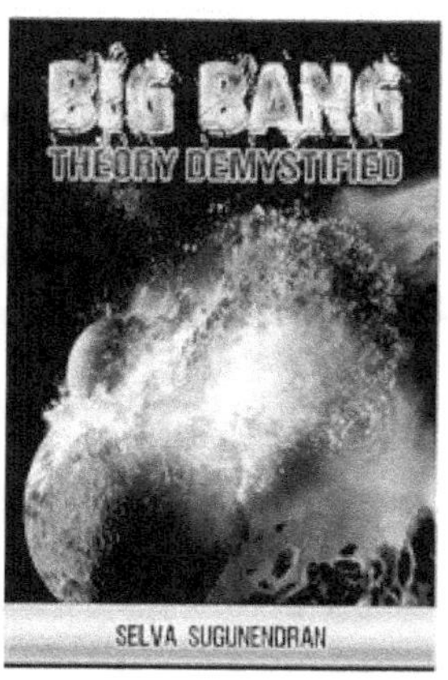

BIG BANG
THEORY DEMYSTIFIED
SELVA SUGUNENDRAN

THE POWER OF DIVINE CONVERSATIONS
UNLOCKING THE SECRETS OF PRAYER
DR. SELVA SUGUNENDRAN

UNANSWERED Prayers
- A JOURNEY OF FAITH
DR. SELVA SUGUNENDRAN

BELIEF BEYOND BOUNDARIES:
EMBRACING THE EXTRAORDINARY THROUGH CHRISTIAN FAITH
By
DR. SELVA SUGUNENDRAN

Appendices

1. WEBSITE LINKS

https://AIRoboticsForGood.com

https://MyChristianLifestyle.org

https://BlessMeLord.com

https://HealMeLord.today

https://CreationEvolutionAndScience.com

https://AIRoboticsForGood.com

https://DementiaAdvice.care

https://HowToLeadAVibrantLifeWithAlzheimers.com

2. CONTACT LINKS:

The Author Email: Selva@MyChristianLifestyle.org

All Books by Author Available on Amazon:

https://selvasmail.com/selvasbooks

www.ingramcontent.com/pod-product-compliance
Lightning Source LLC
Chambersburg PA
CBHW070905250726
48662CB00003B/1517